Marc Phillips

101 SHOOTERS

The Revolutionary Cocktail

Techniques, Recipes & Variations

R&R PUBLISHING

First published in 1992 by
R & R Publishing
12 Treeview Place, Epping, NSW 2121

© R & R Publishing
Marc Phillips

Publisher: Richard Carroll
Production: Stan Carter
Photography: Warren Webb
Photo Assistant: Jon Carroll
Cover Design: Jon Terpstra

All rights reserved. No part of this book may be stored, reproduced or transmitted in any form or by any means without written permission of the publisher, except in the case of brief quotations embodied in critical articles and reviews.

National Library of Australia cataloguing in publication data

Phillips, Marc, 1969 -
Marc Phillips' 101 shooters : the revolutionary cocktail

Includes index.
ISBN: 1 875655 02 6

1. Cocktails. I Title. II. Title: 101 shooters.
III. Title: One hundred and one shooters

641.874

First Edition July, 1992

Computer Typeset in Times Roman by
R & R Publishing
Printed by: Canberra Press

Table of Contents

Introduction	4
Introduction To Responsible Drinking	5
Methods Of Mixing Shooters	5
Techniques For Making Shooters	6
Drinking Methods	7
Helpful Hints	7
Recipe For Cocktail Sauce	8
Ice	8
Chilling Shooters	8
Garnishes	8
Glasses	9
Equipment Required For Shooters	10
Non Alcoholic Ingredients Required	10
Alcohol Needed for Shooter Bars	10
Description Of Liqueurs And Spirits	12
Recipes	17
Acknowledgements	112
Indexes	113
Home User Easy Index	114
Easy Order Form	117

Introduction

The origin of 'shooters' cannot be precisely dated. They evolved as an inexpensive, enjoyable way to 'skol', or consume a drink in one draught. The 'shot' is a standard measure of 30ml and a shot glass was designed to hold this measure. Liqueurs are used to blend with the spirit bases, giving them an enhanced flavour. Through this, shooters have gained their popularity. Kahlua camouflages Tequila's sting, creating the 'Brave Bull'; Sambuca layered with Baileys Irish Cream to relieve the overwhelming aniseed, becomes a 'Slippery Nipple'.

The number of shooter creations has rapidly increased. Many have been fashioned and designed in Melbourne nightclubs, where the shooter has staked its claim as a unique novelty and attraction.

Over the last three years I have performed experiments on numerous spirits and liqueur mixes, noting how the layers occur and change with different arrangements and blends. The Shooter Bar at ZuZu's in Melbourne served as a laboratory for hundreds I created and served.

The best fun from shooters is had in a group where all may experiment with mixing and enjoying the taste sensations without drinking to excess. Moderation is the rule.

Astonishment, bewilderment and laughter were some of the reactions from buyers that led me to write this book. It is about the enjoyment of shooters, mine and yours!

Marc Phillips, June 1992

Introduction To Responsible Drinking

Welcome to "101 Shooters: The Revolutionary Cocktail", where the pleasurable pastime of mixing and drinking delicious cocktails is revived.

Comments on each recipe refer to where, when or for what reason the Shooter is best consumed, which time of day and season, that special occasion (birthday) or just a certain circumstance (after a hard day).

Remember the rules - It is preferable to consume:

ONE SHOOTER PER HOUR

Abiding by this golden rule is essential for your introduction and long term enjoyment of the "Shooter Revolution".

It is always good advice to ask your bar attendant the alcoholic percentage of each Shooter. Their initial recommendation may not always be right for you. If you feel that one Shooter is too strong, try a lighter based Shooter, of which there are a number of suggestions in this book.

It is recommended that you drink a maximum of two or three Shooters in one evening, of various combinations of liqueurs.

Size is misleading. A Shooter glass holds between 30 and 40 ml of ingredients, with most not diluted by water, ice or juice.

The "skoling" or "shooting" drinking action can entice "an easy to drink", syndrome. Treat a Shooter as you would a mixed drink; consume over a reasonable lengthy period of time.

The "Drinking Methods" should be adhered to and be very careful with "Flaming Shooters".

"Shooter Time"

By definition this game ensures Shooters are consumed in a group, as a group. All participants offer a toast to prosperity, good friends and the better things in life. Keep "Shooter Time" surprising and spontaneous.

Overall, I urge you to respect alcohol and protect the establishment of the Shooters identity. I need you to understand that Shooters are a cocktail to be enjoyed not abused.

It is always delightful to mix and enjoy Shooters at home, however if you plan to make a night of it at a friend's home, or in a restaurant, bar, club or hotel, leave the car at home - do not drive and enjoy the experience without worry.

Methods of Mixing Shooters

Only three formal cocktail methods are used to mix shooters. No shooters are 'shaken' or 'blended'. Most are constructed by 'building', several are 'poured' and a few are 'stirred'.

1. Building: This method is synonymous with layering, the drink is built or layered in ascending levels. With only a few exceptions, shooters are made this way; all levels being visibly distinct.

2. Pouring: Without the assistance of any implement, apart from a free pourer if one is available, the ingredients are 'poured' directly from the bottle into the glass.

3. Stirring: This is the slow, cyclical movement, using a straw or swizzle stick that mixes the ingredients.

Techniques for making shooters

1. Layering: The easiest way to keep the alcoholic ingredients separate is to use a spoon. Hold the spoon right way up and rest it with the lip of its rim slightly above the level of of the last layer. Fill the spoon gently and the contents will flow smoothly from all around the rim. Use the back of the spoon's dish only if you are experienced and feel comfortable with it.

If you don't have a spoon handy, holding two straws together will provide an adequate alternative. In a busy bar or at a party, straws are usually around in numbers while your spoons are easily misplaced, or in need of cleaning. Once you are adept at layering, any implement with a flat surface will suffice; like a knife or a swizzle stick.

2. Tilting: Holding the glass on a 45° angle and pouring gently, but directly, from the bottle will form an even flow down the inside of the glass and onto the previous layer. You may gain assistance using a 'free pourer', or 'measured pourer', fitted to bottles. Tilting is very efficient for some mixes, and faster than layering over a spoon. Baileys Irish Cream, lends itself well to layering by tilting.

3. Lighting: Use a match in preference to a lighter and ignite the flammable alcohol from the rim ensuring your hand is not protruding into the area of the naked flame. Green Chartreuse and Bundaberg Overproof Rum will ignite immediately whereas Yellow Chartreuse and Sambuca may require relighting or applying the light for longer.

4. Floating: This technique is used for the finishing layer of cream or lemon juice. I recommend a plastic nozzle-tipped bottle that will evenly spread these ingredients. Apply in a circular motion.

5. Slamming: When a soft-drink mixer is used the technique of slamming will produce a fizzy effect. Cup your hand right over the glass, lift it and 'slam' the base onto the bar or any level surface.

6. Dash: A dash is exactly that! It is a small quantity added to a drink to give a certain colour or flavour effect. It is used seldom in shooters.

7. Pouring: This is the simplest of all techniques and will not create layers, though the various ingredients will separate themselves to give a multi-coloured appearance. Higher percentage volume alcohols should be 'poured' into lower percentage alcohols. When pouring straight from the bottle you must take care to add the right quantities. If you have limited experience, use a pourer with a measure. If experienced, use a free pourer to enable the right quantity to evenly and smoothly flow into glass. Pour just above surface of the drink and in the centre of the glass to prevent splashing on the sides, which mars the look and appeal of the shooter.

8. Stirring: As most shooters are layered stirring is optional. Some prefer their shooter not be stirred. For an individual drink three to five slow rotations with a swizzle stick, straw or spoon handle is adequate. If you are making a batch to be stored for use during a party or in a busy bar then regularly stirring is recommended to prevent separation of the ingredients.

9. Dropping: This technique is used to gain the affect of a 'tear drop' in the centre of a shooter. Submerge one third of a straw into the milk, spirit or liqueur you wish to use, cover the open end of the straw with your index finger and lift from the liquid. Rest ten millimetres above the centre of the shooter's surface, momentarily release finger to drop the liquid into the shooter. Alternatively an eye dropper or pipette may be used.

Drinking Methods

1. Shoot: This technique, called 'skoling' in some parts of the world, derives its name from a 'shot' — a standard 30ml nip of alcohol served in a small 'shot' glass. It also describes the drinking action of throwing the drink quickly into your mouth. The taste and pleasure comes from holding the drink on your tongue. Shooting, rather than sipping, yields the blended characteristics of shooters.

2. Straw Shoot: Take a straw and put it in the shooter, with its tip to the bottom of the glass, draw up the contents. Any shooter may be drunk with a straw.

3. Shoot While Flaming: Leave five millimetres from the top of the glass free of alcohol. After lighting, leave the flame burning for 10 to 15 seconds. The flame will always extinguish before touching any skin, but do not rest the rim of the glass on your lower lip as it may be quite warm. The flame may be extinguished before shooting. If you opt for this method the warmth of the shooter is still maintained by allowing the flame to burn a little longer, for 15 to 30 seconds before extinguishing. If you elect to shoot a flaming shooter with a straw allow the flame to burn from 15 to 30 seconds. This will warm the shot glass without altering the drink. Insert the straw to the bottom of the glass. As the shooter is consumed from the bottom layer to the top the temperature gradually increases. If you wish to straw shoot without the flame, keep the ingredients alight for longer, up to 60 seconds, before extinguishing to achieve a similar effect.

4. Tandem: Two people place their straws into the shooter and straw shoot. This method is for enjoyment of drinking partners or for going 'Dutch'. Especially suitable for 'Spanish Flies' and 'Double Dates'.

5. Lick Sip Suck: This famous method yields the utmost enjoyment from Tequila. On the flat piece of skin between the base of your thumb and index finger, place a pinch of salt. Place a quarter of a lemon by you on the bar. Lick the salt off your hand, shoot the Tequila and then suck the slice of lemon. Delicious!

6. Suction Straw Shoot: Place the tip of your straw below the first layer of alcohol. Draw the top layer first, then submerge straw to next level and repeat process, and so on to the bottom layer. Great for 'Suction Cups' & 'Traffic Lights'.

Helpful Hints

Here are a few pointers. Do not drink too many shooters too quickly. Shooters are deceptive. Because of their small size and the novelty of making and drinking them some people do not consider the end result. One per hour is a maximum for most people, take a long soft drink or light beer between shooters to pace yourself.

A) Don't overly concern yourself with exact divisions of alcohol layers. Baileys will plonk into Sambuca, rise and sit decisively upon it whereas Grand Marnier can be practically impossible to layer every time if you are not experienced.

B) Leaving the spoon used in layering in a glass filled with soda water will clean off the alcohol.

C) Floating cream is easier and gives a better appearance if a 'nozzle-tipped' plastic bottle is used. With a circular motion, swirls of cream rest upon the alcohol. Leave the bottle out of the refrigerator for 5-10 minutes to soften the cream. This assists a smooth flow and avoids lumps and blobs.

D) Lastly, you should experiment. Spirits with higher alcohol levels layer upon spirits with lower alcohol levels. Vary combinations by substituting and replacing spirits and liqueurs as you wish, watch for the effects being created.

Recipe for Cocktail Sauce: This sauce is used for the Oyster Shooter and you should always have a supply at your bar. It is best kept chilled in a jug or bottle. Mix ingredients by stirring first, then semi-whip by hand with a tablespoon. This recipe makes 100ml.

    3 tablespoons of cream
    3 tablespoons of tomato sauce
    1/2 tablespoon of Worcestershire sauce
    5ml Milne Brandy

Ice: Though ice is not required in shooters some people will express a preference. In such a case I suggest crushed ice, sprinkled on the shooter. To crush ice, fold some into a clean linen cloth and strike it against a solid wall or the floor.

Chilling: Shooters, particularly those containing lemon juice, should be served chilled. Refrigerated lemon juice chills the alcohol when floated on the shooter. If the lemon juice is warm a sprinkling of crushed ice will cool the shooter, increasing its refreshing qualities. Storing glasses in the refrigerator takes away the need to use ice. A blender may be used for small quantities, but is a rather slow method.

Garnishes: The distinctive difference between cocktails and shooters is the absence of garnishes in the latter. Generally, cocktails are a single colour or layer, requiring fruit, plastic animals, umbrellas or scattered spices to identify the drink and its style. The essence of the shooter revolution is the attractive, distinct layering of the ingredients. Appeal, both to the eye and the palate, is dependent on this separation of ingredients.

Garnishing shooters is unnecessary and impractical for most drinking methods. Show off your shooter by employing the best mixing method for greatest appeal. The exceptions are; 'Flaming Sambuca', which has three coffee beans and; shooters containing Kahlua, Bailey's Irish Cream, Frangelico, Tia Maria or cream may be sprinkled with cinnamon, chocolate flakes or nutmeg.

Glasses: The use of shot glasses is a crucial aspect of the shooter revolution. There are different styles of shot glasses, from squat to stemmed, each lending themselves to particular shooter presentations. Libbey, manufacture a range of glasses that are ideal for most shooters. Their glasses will be referred to in the book for consistency and are; Whisky Shot, Cordial (Lexington), Cordial (Embassy) and Tall Dutch Cordial.

Whisky Shot: This is a traditional 'shot' glass. This hard-based glass conjures images of short, sharp shooting spirits and liqueurs. It holds 45ml when full.

Cordial (Lexington): This mature, elegant glass with its high neck and long stem magnifies its contents, unusually novel in a shooter. It holds 37ml when full.

Cordial (Embassy): This is a wider-rimmed glass, yet its concise parameters may house a multitude of shooters, from flaming to traditional. It holds 30ml when full.

Tall Dutch Cordial: Prestigious in appearance, this glass reigns supreme when you are defining different, colourful layers in a shooter. It holds 45ml when full.

Wine Goblet: For the 'Sambuca Shaker' you will require a 140ml wine goblet with a rim that will fit inside the palm of your hand. If the rim is too large it is difficult to achieve any suction, the same applies if the rim is too small.

Glassware Hints: The following hints will help you gain the best effects from your glassware. Frosted and misty effects are achieved by simply running glasses under cold water then refrigerating or freezing them. Glasses without engravings, designs or colours create clearer visual representations. Hand-washing glasses is preferable to dishwashing machines especially for removing cream, dense liqueurs or dried fragments of lemon juice and cream. Be adventurous when experimenting with shooters in various glasses.

Equipment Required for Shooters

Bottle Opener
Dropper (Pipette)
Free Pourers
Jugs
Knife (Small paring type)
Linen Cloths
Matches

Mixing Bowl
Measures (Jiggers)
Nozzle-Tipped Plastic Bottle
Straws (Long and Short)
Swizzle Sticks
Tablespoons
Teaspoons

Non Alcoholic Ingredients Required for Shooters

Black Coffee
Cinnamon
Chilli Red Pepper
Chocolate Flakes
Coffee Beans
Cream
Dry Ginger Ale
Egg White
Grenadine
Ice
Lemonade
Lemons
Lemon Juice

Lime Cordial/Juice
Milk
Nutmeg
Orange Juice
Oysters
Raspberry Cordial
Salt
Soda Water
Tobasco Sauce
Tomato Juice
Tomato Sauce
Worcestershire Sauce

Alcohol Needed for Shooter Bars

The list on the following page, is a complete range of the alcoholic ingredients used in this book. Most bars will have such a range, whereas a home shooter bar may be more limited. You will be able to experiment with ingredients to replace those on this list and for which you have a similar or replacement brand. The shooters in this book have been tested using the brands listed.

For ease of locating required ingredients, go to the indexes at the back of the book. Drinks are listed there by name, alternative name and spirit or liqueur used in the drink.

Alcohol recommended for a cocktail bar (And used for testing recipes in this book)

Spirits
Gin - Gilbey's
Gin - Seagram's
Vodka - Finlandia
Vodka - Karloff
Vodka - Smirnoff
Apricot Brandy
Canadian Club
Brandy - Milne
Brandy - Chatelle Napoleon
Bundaberg OP Rum
Jack Daniels
Peachtree Schnapps
Tullamore Dew Irish Whisky
Scotch - Ballantines
Scotch - The Black Douglas
Bourbon - Cougar
Bourbon - Early Times
Coruba Jamaican Rum
Tequila - El Toro
Tequila - Pepe Lopez
Aphrodite Ouzo
Southern Comfort
Campari
Pernod
Malibu

Liqueurs
Baileys
Grand Marnier
Tia Maria
Kahlua
Cointreau
Galliano
Amaretto di Saronno
Dom Benedictine

Liqueurs
Sambuca - di Galliano
Sambuca - Opal Nera
Sambuca - Romana
Sambuca - Seagram's
Lochan Ora
Frangelico Hazelnut Liqueur
Mango Liqueur
Vandermint
Sabra
Midori
Parfait Amour
Green Chartreuse
Yellow Chartreuse

Seagram's Liqueurs
Banana
Peach
Strawberry
Blue Curacao
Orange Curacao
Triple Sec
Kirsch
Coconut
Melon
Cassis
Dark Creme de Cacao
White Creme de Cacao
Creme de Menthe Green
Creme de Menthe White
Advocaat
Cherry Advocaat
Cherry Brandy

Vermouth
Cinzano Rosso Vermouth
Cinzano Dry Vermouth
Cinzano Bianco Vermouth
Campari

Description of Liqueurs and Spirits

General Comments on Seagram Liqueurs

The whole range of these liqueurs, traditional or modern, is based on **natural**, imported and locally produced flavouring. In some cases these ingredients are very costly, but for sake of a top-quality finished product alternatives are not used.

Advocaat: A combination of fresh egg whites, yokes, sugar, brandy and spirit. Using natural vanilla makes the product unique, and equal or better than any well-known brand from Europe.
Banana : The flavour of fresh, ripe bananas is the perfect base for the definitive daiquiri and a host of other exciting fruit cocktails.
Cassis: Another natural based new product of Seagram. Deep, rich purple promises and delivers a regal and robust flavour and aroma. Cassis lends itself to neat drinking or an endless array of delicious sauces and desserts.
Cherry Advocaat: Same as Advocaat, plus natural cherry flavours are added.
Cherry Brandy: Is made from concentrated, imported morello cherry juice. (The only fruit which does not grow in Australia.) Small quantity of bitter almonds and vanilla is added to make it more enjoyable as a neat drink before or after dinner. Excellent for mixers, topping, ice cream, fruit salads, pancakes, etc.
Coconut: A smooth liqueur, composed of exotic coconut, heightened with light-bodied white rum. Delightful on the rocks, combine with other Seagram Liqueurs to create exciting cocktails.
Creme de Cacao Dark: Rich, deep chocolate that only the best quality ingredients supply. Smooth and classy. Serve on its own, or mix for all kinds of delectable treats.
Creme de Cacao White: Seagram proves you can't judge by its colour. Mysteriously clear, this liqueur delivers a powerfully lively, full bodied chocolate flavour. Excellent ingredient when absence of colour is desired.
Creme de Menthe Green: Made from the best available ingredients in the world. Clear peppermint flavour, reminiscent of a fresh, crisp, clean winter's day in the mountains. Excellent mixer, a necessity in the gourmet kitchen.
Creme de Menthe White: As Creme de Menthe Green, when colour is not desired.
Curacao Blue: Same as Triple Sec, brilliant blue colour is added to make some cocktails more exciting.
Curacao Orange: Again, same as above, but stronger in orange, colouring is used for other varieties of cocktail mixers.

Curacao Tripe Sec: Based on natural citrus fruits. Well known fact is citrus fruits are the most important aromatic flavour constituents. Interesting to know citrus fruit was known 2,000 years before Christ. As a liqueur one of the most versatile. Can be enjoyed with or without ice as a neat drink, or used in mixed cocktails more than any other liqueur. Triple Sec - also known as White Curacao.

Kirsch: A fruit brandy distilled from morello cherries. Delicious drunk straight and excellent in a variety of food recipes.

Melon: Soft green, exudes freshness. Refreshing and mouth-watering honeydew melon. Simple yet complex. Smooth on the palate, serve on the rocks, or use to create summertime cocktails.

Peach: The flavour of fresh peaches and natural peach juice make this cocktail lover's dream.

Pineapple: A just ripe, sun-filled delight. Plucked from Queensland fields, fresh ingredients deliver succulent true-to-the fruit aroma and flavour. Delicious neat, a necessity for summertime cocktails.

Sambuca: Don't let its subtle appearance fool you. Prepare yourself for an electrifying taste experience. Based on the very "stimulating" ancient aniseed extract. Neat or mixed, add new dimension to "espresso".

Strawberry: Striking, fluorescent red, unmistakable strawberry bouquet. This natural liqueur delivers a true to nature, fresh strawberry flavour. Ideal for neat drinking, Seagram's Strawberry Liqueur lends itself to mixing and culinary creations.

Other Liqueurs

Amaretto Di Saronno: A rich subtle liqueur with a unique almond flavour. Still made to a secret recipe devised in 1525, this is the original Amaretto.

Baileys Irish Cream: The largest selling liqueur in the world, was introduced onto the Australian market in 1974. It is a blend of Irish Whisky, softened by Irish Cream and other flavourings. It is a natural product.

Benadictine: A perfect end to a perfect meal. Serve straight, with ice, soda, or as part of a favourite cocktail.

Campari: A drink for many occasions, both as a long or short drink, or as a key ingredient in many fashionable cocktails.

Chartreuse: A liqueur available in either yellow or green colour. Made by the monks of the Carthusian order. The only world famous liqueur still made by monks.

Cointreau: Made from a neutral grain spirit, as opposed to Cognac. An aromatic flavour of natural citrus fruits. A great mixer or delightful over ice.

Creme de Grand Marnier: A blend of Grand Marnier and smooth French cream. A premium product, a very smooth taste with the orange/cognac flavour blending beautifully with smooth cream. Introduced to Australia in 1985.

Drambuie: A Scotch Whisky liqueur. Made from a secret recipe dating back to 1745. "Dram Buidheach" the drink that satisfies.

Frangelico: A precious liqueur imported from Italy. Made from wild Hazel-nuts with infusions of berries and flowers to enrich the flavour.
Galliano: The distinguished taste! A classic liqueur that blends with a vast array of mixed drinks.
Grand Marnier: An original blend of fine old Cognac and an extract of oranges. The recipe is over 150 years old
Kahlua: A smooth, dark liqueur made from real coffee and fine clear spirits. Its origins are based in Mexico.
Lochan Ora: Based on a subtle blend of premium scotch whisky, honey, curacao and anise, Lochan Ora is an after dinner delight.
Malibu: A clear liqueur based on white rum with the subtle addition of coconut. Its distinctive taste blends naturally with virtually every mixer available.
Passoa: A spirit based passionfruit drink. Serve well chilled, neat or mixed. Passoa mixes extremely well with fruit juices.
Peachtree Schnapps: Crystal clear, light liqueur, bursting with the taste of ripe peaches. Drink chilled or on the rocks or mix with any soft drink or juice.
Sabra: A unique flavour which comes from tangy jaffa oranges, with a hint of chocolate.
Sambuca Romana: The largest selling international Sambuca. It was the first ever produced and is fully imported from Italy. Only recently launched in Australia.
Southern Comfort: A liqueur not a bourbon as often thought. It is unique, full-bodied liquor with a touch of sweetness. Its recipe is a secret, but it is known to be based on peaches and apricots. It is the largest selling liqueur in Australia.
Tia Maria: A liqueur with a cane spirit base, and its flavour derived from the finest Jamaican coffee. It is not too sweet with a subtle taste of coffee.
Vandermint: A rich chocolate liqueur with the added zest of mint.

Spirits
Bourbon
Cougar: A smooth, mellow bourbon since 1865.
Early Times: The second largest selling Bourbon in the USA and Japan. Its smooth quality makes it ideal for cocktails or for drinking straight.
Brandy
Martell Cognac: The art of Martell, a distinctive flavoured cognac with an elegant roundness.
Chatelle Napoleon: 100% French brandy, smooth and mellow, it represents cognac quality at a brandy price.
Milne: Smooth and mild Australian spirit, is considered a very smooth and palatable brandy, ideal for mixing.
Gin
Gilbey's: The number one selling Gin in Australia. Its aroma comes from using the highest quality juniper berries and other rare and subtle herbs. Perfect mixer for both short and long drinks.

Seagram's London Dry: A crisp, clean gin with botanical formulation distilled from a 100% grain.

Ouzo:

Aphrodite: The traditional spirit aperitif of Greece. The distinctive flavour is derived mainly from the seed of the anise plant. A neutral grain spirit, flavoured with anise and distilled in Australia.

Rum

Bacardi: A smooth, dry, light bodied rum, especially suited for drinks in which you require subtle aroma and delicate flavour.

Bacardi Gold: Matured in charred oak barrels to give a dry smooth taste and a clear golden colour. Use in Bacardi drinks where you want a fuller, mellow flavour.

Bundaberg: The most popular Australian rum, mixes well with all juices and splits.

Captain Morgan White Label: A light-bodied, smooth rum that is a perfect mixer in long drinks.

Coruba: A dark blended Jamaican Rum, made from both pot still and continuous stilled rums. Smooth and mellow, aged relatively longer than other international rums.

Rye Whisky:

Canadian Club: The largest selling Canadian whisky in North America and Australia. Distilled from corn, rye and malted barley. A light, mild and delicate whisky, ideal for drinking straight or in mixed cocktails.

Scotch Whisky

Ballantines: One of the top three Scotch Whiskies in the world. It is a blended whisky and is one of the very few "bottled in Scotland" products available in Australia.

Unlike most other Scotches, it is 40% alc/vol as opposed to 37.2% alc/vol, which enhances the whisky flavour.

The Black Douglas: A blend of quality scotch whiskies, aged for a minimum of eight years. A Scotch with great flavour that is smoother and mellower on the palate.

Tennessee Whisky:

Jack Daniel's: Contrary to popular belief, Jack Daniel's is not a bourbon, it is a distinctive product called Tennessee Whisky. Made from the 'old sour mash' process. Leached through hard maple charcoal very slowly. Then aged in charred white oak barrels, at a controlled temperature, acquiring its body, bouquet and colour, yet remaining smooth.

Tequila

El Toro: A clear tequila imported from Mexico, with a scented, clean character and slight burn, perfect for drinking straight, also a great mixer.

Pepe Lopez: Distilled from the Mexcal variety of the agave plant - not Cacti. Pepe Lopez was named after a 19th Century Mexican bandit. A perfect mixer or drink straight with salt and lemon.

Vodka
Finlandia: From Finland's purest, natural spring water, using the most advanced distiling techniques in the world. Renowned internationally for its superbly smooth taste.
Karloff: Double distiled and passed through charcoal filters, has the unobtrusive flavour and bouquet that makes it the perfect mixer.
Smirnoff: The second largest selling spirit in the world and the leading Vodka in the world including Australia. Most Vodkas are steeped in tanks containing charcoal, but Smirnoff is pumped through ten columns of best hardwood charcoal for seven hours, removing all odours and impurities, making a superior quality product

Angostura Bitters:
An essential part of any bar or kitchen. A unique additive whose origins date back to 1824. A mysterious blend of natural herbs and spices, both a seasoning and flavouring agent, in both sweet and savoury dishes and drinks. Ideal for dieters as it is low in sodium and calories.

Vermouth:
By description, Vermouth is a herbally infused wine. The base wine used is grown and manufactured in Griffith, NSW, and is of such high quality, that Australian Cinzano is recognised as the best in the world.
Three Cinzano styles are most prevalent, these are:
Rosso: A bitter sweet herbal flavour and is often drunk as an aperitif.
Bianco: Is light, fruity and refreshing. Mixes well with soda, lemonade and fruit juices.
Dry: Is crisp, light and dry and is used as a base for many cocktails.

ALABAMA SLAMMER

METHOD: Pour in order

GLASS: Whisky Shot

INGREDIENTS:

    10ml Seagram's London Dry Gin
    10ml Amaretto di Saronno
    10ml Orange Juice
    15ml Southern Comfort

TECHNIQUE: Shoot

COMMENTS: A real drink! From the heart of the Deep South, U.S.A.

ATOMIC BOMB

METHOD: Layer in order, then float cream

GLASS: Tall Dutch Cordial

INGREDIENTS:

20ml Tia Maria
15ml Seagram's London Dry Gin
10ml Cream

TECHNIQUE: Shoot

COMMENTS: A strategic 'one shooter weapon', this drink explodes down the unsuspecting throat. Delicious in emergencies! Gin may be replaced with Cointreau, or Seagram's Triple Sec.

B & B SHOOTER

METHOD: Pour in order.

GLASS: Cordial (Lexington)

INGREDIENTS:

    18ml Martell Cognac
       or Chatelle Napoleon Brandy
    18ml DOM Benedictine

TECHNIQUE: Shoot

COMMENTS: For mature drinkers! Grandpa can turn up the pace of his medication. The Shooter is quick and smooth, the traditional B & B cocktail is normally served in a brandy baloon.

B-52 SHOOTER

METHOD: Layer in order.

GLASS: Cordial (Embassy)

INGREDIENTS:

    10ml Kahlua
    10ml Cointreau
    10ml Baileys Irish Cream

TECHNIQUE: Shoot

COMMENTS: This sweet, blended shot is usually sipped. Cointreau is often replaced with Grand Marnier. Also see 'KGB'. Not to be confused with the traditional B-52 cocktail, which has greater volume, is built over ice and usually served in a 140ml Old Fashioned Spirit Glass.

BEE STING

METHOD: Layer in order, then light.

GLASS: Cordial (Embassy)

INGREDIENTS:

    20ml El Toro Tequila
    10ml Yellow Chartreuse

TECHNIQUE: Straw shoot while flaming.

COMMENTS: Ouch! The Yellow Chartreuse attacks your throat with a numbing, pleasurable pain, as Tequila buzzes you back to the party. Drink quickly so the straw won't melt!

BLACK RUSSIAN SHOOTER

METHOD: Layer in order.

GLASS: Cordial (Embassy)

INGREDIENTS:
15ml Kahlua
15ml Smirnoff Vodka

TECHNIQUE: Shoot

COMMENTS: Superb after dinner as the Smirnoff Vodka lubricates the way for the scrumptious chocolate topping. Tia Maria or Dark Creme de Cacao may be substituted for Kahlua, making the drink a "Black Pearl".
The traditicnal Black Russian cocktail has greater volume, is built over ice and served in a 210ml Old Fashioned Spirit Glass.

BLOOD BATH

METHOD: Pour in order then layer the Pepe Lopez Tequila.

GLASS: Whisky Shot

INGREDIENTS:

10ml Cinzano Rosso Vermouth
15ml Seagram's Strawberry Liqueur
20ml Pepe Lopez Tequila

TECHNIQUE: Shoot

COMMENTS: Cherry grins and rosy cheeks characterise the after effects of this blood thirsty experience. Only issued after midnight and before dawn!

BLOW JOB

METHOD: Layer in order.

GLASS: Cordial (Lexington)

INGREDIENTS:

25ml Green Creme de Menthe
12ml Baileys Irish Cream

TECHNIQUE: Shoot

COMMENTS: A light minty confectionery flavour and creamy texture provide a mouthful for those who indulge. Twist this to a "Rattlesnake" by adding Green Chartreuse.

BRAIN DAMAGE

METHOD: Layer the Parfait Amour and Malibu, then pour the Advocaat.

GLASS: Cordial (Lexington)

INGREDIENTS:

22ml Malibu
10ml Parfait Amour
5ml Seagram's Advocaat

TECHNIQUE: Shoot

COMMENTS: Separation induces restless nights, Advocaat intervenes to mould the senses.

BRAVE BULL

METHOD: Layer in order.

GLASS: Whisky Shot

INGREDIENTS:
30ml Kahlua
15ml Pepe Lopez Tequila

TECHNIQUE: Shoot

COMMENTS: One of my favourites for late night revellers, will resist fatique and maintain stamina. Add Aphrodite Ouzo and a "TKO" is punched out.

CALYPSO

METHOD: Layer in order

GLASS: Tall Dutch Cordial

INGREDIENTS:
15ml Baileys Irish Cream
10ml Malibu
20ml Coruba Rum

TECHNIQUE: Shoot

COMMENTS: A Calypso mood, created by Malibu Coconut and Baileys Irish Cream.

CHASTITY BELT

METHOD: Layer in order, then float the cream.

GLASS: Tall Dutch Cordial

INGREDIENTS:

20ml Tia Maria
10ml Frangelico Hazelnut Liqueur
10ml Baileys Irish Cream
 5ml Cream

TECHNIQUE: Shoot

COMMENTS: Morality implores you not to succumb to the super-sweet delicacys of drinkings perversity.

CHERRY RIPE

METHOD: Layer in order.

GLASS: Cordial (Embassy)

INGREDIENTS:
10ml Kahlua
10ml Seagram's Cherry Advocaat
10ml Cinzano Rosso Vermouth

TECHNIQUE: Shoot

COMMENTS: More a dessert than a drink, it was originally made with Strawberry (Rubis) Suntory and Baileys Irish Cream. Take your pick!

CHILLI SHOT

METHOD: Pour

GLASS: Whisky Shot

INGREDIENTS:

45ml Smirnoff Vodka
Slice of red chilli pepper

TECHNIQUE: Shoot

COMMENTS: Feeling mischievous? Refrigerate the Vodka with one red chilli pepper (or 3 to 5 drops of Tabasco sauce) for 24 hours before serving.

CHOCOLATE NOUGAT

METHOD: Pour in order then layer the Baileys Irish Cream.

GLASS: Cordial (Embassy)

INGREDIENTS:

10ml Frangelico Hazelnut Liqueur
10ml DOM Benedictine
10ml Baileys Irish Cream

TECHNIQUE: Shoot

COMMENTS: A swirling pleasure zone of flowing Baileys Irish Cream, above the finest Benedictine and based with voluptious hazelnuts, accentuating the meaning of chocolate.

COATHANGER

METHOD: Layer Pepe Lopez Tequila onto the Cointreau, dash Cordial or Grenadine, then drop the milk.

GLASS: Cordial (Lexington)

INGREDIENTS:

15ml Cointreau
15ml Pepe Lopez Tequila
 7ml Grenadine or Raspberry cordial
Drop of milk

TECHNIQUE: Shoot, then cup hand entirely over the rim, insert straw between fingers into the glass and inhale fumes.

COMMENTS: A euphoric experience, quiet stunning to your senses.

COURTING PENELOPE

METHOD: Pour in order

GLASS: Cordial (Lexington)

INGREDIENTS:
22ml Martell Cognac
15ml Grand Marnier

TECHNIQUE: Shoot

COMMENTS: A distinctive acquired taste is needed for two inseparable moments!

DARK SUNSET

METHOD: Layer in order

GLASS: Tall Dutch Cordial

INGREDIENTS:
>22ml Seagram's Dark Creme de Cacao
>22ml Malibu

TECHNIQUE: Shoot

COMMENTS: This tropical paradise reflects sunset, beaches and the ripe coconuts of Malibu.

DEVIL'S HANDBRAKE

METHOD: Layer in order.

GLASS: Tall Dutch Cordial

INGREDIENTS:

15ml Seagram's Banana Liqueur
15ml Mango Liqueur
15ml Seagram's Cherry Brandy

TECHNIQUE: Shoot

COMMENTS: A magnificent bounty of fruit infiltrated by the devil. Exquisite after a swim

DIRTY ORGASM

METHOD: Layer in order.

GLASS: Tall Dutch Cordial

INGREDIENTS:
> 15ml Cointreau*
> 15ml Galliano
> 15ml Baileys Irish Cream

TECHNIQUE: Shoot

COMMENTS: The Irish frolic between the world's two best lovers, Italian Galliano and French Cointreau. Also known as a 'Screaming Orgasm'. Drambuie may replace Galliano.

* Cointreau may be substituted with Seagram's Triple Sec (as photographed)

DOUBLE DATE

METHOD: Layer in order.

GLASS: Tall Dutch Cordial

INGREDIENTS:
    15ml Seagram's Melon Liqueur
    15ml Seagram's White Creme de Menthe
    15ml DOM Benedictine

TECHNIQUE: Tandem

COMMENTS: Soothing Creme de Menthe restrains the passion of DOM and Melon. For romantics.

FIZZY RUSH

METHOD: Pour in order.

GLASS: Tall Dutch Cordial

INGREDIENTS:

    5ml Seagram's White Creme de Menthe
    10ml Apricot Brandy
    30ml Champagne

TECHNIQUE: Shoot

COMMENTS: Bubbles of refreshing Apricot guaranteed to get up your nose.

FLAMING LAMBORGHINI SHOOTER

METHOD: Layer in order, then light.

GLASS: Cordial (Embassy)

INGREDIENTS:

10ml Kahlua
10ml Galliano
10ml Green Chartreuse

TECHNIQUE: Shoot while flaming.

COMMENTS: Get the party into motion. Essential for birthday celebrants.

FLAMING LOVER

METHOD: Pour Triple Sec over lit Sambuca while drinking through a straw

GLASS: Cordial (Embassy)

INGREDIENTS:
15ml Seagram's Sambuca
15ml Seagram's Triple Sec

TECHNIQUE: Straw shoot while flaming

COMMENTS: The Triple Sec softens the flame for inexperienced drinkers of flaming shooters.

FLAMING SAMBUCA

METHOD: Pour Sambuca Romana, float coffee beans and light.

GLASS: Cordial (Embassy)

INGREDIENTS:

    30ml Sambuca Romana
    3 Coffee Beans

TECHNIQUE: Shoot after flame extinguished.

COMMENTS: Provides relief from the cold winter. The other way we do it, is to pour Sambuca into a wine glass then light. Cup your hand entirely over the rim while it flames, creating suction. Shake the glass, place under your nose, take your hand from the glass to inhale the fumes, then shoot!

FREDDIE FUD PUCKER

METHOD: Layer El Toro Tequila onto Galliano then drop Orange Curacao

GLASS: Cordial (Lexington)

INGREDIENTS:

22ml Galliano
10ml El Toro Tequila
 5ml Seagram's Orange Curacao

TECHNIQUE: Shoot

COMMENTS: Known to induce dancing on bars and at beach parties, be sure to mind your 'p's and 'f's when ordering.

FRUIT TINGLE

METHOD: Layer in order, optional to stir.

GLASS: Cordial (Embassy)

INGREDIENTS:

    10ml Seagram's Blue Curacao
    15ml Mango Liqueur
    5ml Lemon juice

TECHNIQUE: Shoot

COMMENTS: Tangy and piquant. Seagram's Melon Liqueur may be substituted for Mango Liqueur

GALLIANO HOT SHOT

METHOD: Top Galliano with black coffee, then float cream.

GLASS: Tall Dutch Cordial

INGREDIENTS:

15ml Galliano
25ml Black Coffee
 5ml Cream

TECHNIQUE: Shoot

COMMENTS: When in a hurry, a great way to enjoy a liqueur coffee.

G.A.S.

METHOD: Layer the Galliano onto Sambuca and pour Amaretto.

GLASS: Cordial (Embassy)

INGREDIENTS:
>10ml Sambuca di Galliano
>10ml Galliano
>10ml Amaretto di Galliano

TECHNIQUE: Shoot

COMMENTS: A fun and tasty liqueur mix. A specialty developed for the Galliano Company.

GOLDEN CADILLAC SHOOTER

METHOD: Layer Galliano and White Creme de Cacao, then float cream.

GLASS: Tall Dutch Cordial

INGREDIENTS:
15ml Seagram's White Creme de Cacao
20ml Galliano
10ml Cream

TECHNIQUE: Shoot

COMMENTS: Comfort in style is what the distilled cocoa beans give golden Galliano - a real dazzler! The traditional Golden Cadillac cocktail has a larger volume, is shaken over ice and served in a 140ml Champagne Saucer.

GREEK GOD

METHOD: Pour in order.

GLASS: Whisky Shot

INGREDIENTS:
22ml Aphrodite Ouzo
22ml Pernod

TECHNIQUE: Shoot

COMMENTS: Appease the gods by drinking their aniseed aphrodisiac.

GREEN SLIME

METHOD: Pour in order, then stir.

GLASS: Whisky Shot

INGREDIENTS:

20ml Seagram's Melon Liqueur
15ml Karloff Vodka
5ml Egg White

TECHNIQUE: Shoot.

COMMENTS: Add more egg white for greater slime. Melon will keep the taste buds occupied, Vodka dilutes the egg white.

HALF NELSON

METHOD: Layer in order.

GLASS: Whisky Shot

INGREDIENTS:
> 15ml Seagram's Green Creme de Menthe
> 10ml Seagram's Strawberry Liqueur
> 20ml Grand Marnier

TECHNIQUE: Shoot

COMMENTS: The referee is unable to break the grip of Strawberry locking its green opponent into an immovable position. For the temporarily incapacitated.

HARBOUR LIGHTS

METHOD: Layer in order.

GLASS: Cordial (Lexington)

INGREDIENTS:

12ml Kahlua
12ml Seagram's Sambuca
12ml Green Chartreuse

TECHNIQUE: Straw shoot

COMMENTS: Glittering reflections sparkle on the harbour beside a candlelight dinner. Substitute Yellow Chartreuse if preferred.

HARD ON

METHOD: Layer Seagram's Banana Liqueur onto Kahlua, then float the cream.

GLASS: Tall Dutch Cordial

INGREDIENTS:

20ml Kahlua
15ml Seagram's Banana Liqueur
10ml Cream

TECHNIQUE: Shoot

COMMENTS: The first to float cream, voted the most popular shooter.

HELLRAISER

METHOD: Layer in order.

GLASS: Whisky Shot

INGREDIENTS:

15ml Midori
15ml Strawberry (Rubis) Suntory
15ml Opal Nera

TECHNIQUE: Shoot

COMMENTS: The latest shooter from the Suntory Company, using Opal Nera, the Black Sambuca.

HIGH AND DRY

METHOD: Pour in order, then stir.

GLASS: Cordial (Embassy)

INGREDIENTS:
10ml Cinzano Bianco Vermouth
15ml Pepe Lopez Tequila
5ml Cinzano Dry Vermouth

TECHNIQUE: Shoot

COMMENTS: Disguise the mischief of Pepe Lopez Tequila with Cinzano Dry Vermouth. Best served chilled.

INKAHLUARABLE

METHOD: Layer in order.

GLASS: Cordial (Embassy)

INGREDIENTS:

    10ml Kahlua
    10ml Seagram's Triple Sec
    10ml Grand Marnier

TECHNIQUE: Shoot

COMMENTS: Terminal illness can be momentarily postponed with this Kahlua-based antidote.

IRISH FLAG

METHOD: Layer in order.

GLASS: Cordial (Lexington)

INGREDIENTS:
12ml Seagram's Green Creme de Menthe
12ml Baileys Irish Cream
12ml Chatelle Napoleon Brandy

TECHNIQUE: Shoot

COMMENTS: A stroll through verdant pastures. Brandy may be replaced with Tullamore Dew — an Old Irish Whisky.

ITALIAN STALLION

METHOD: Pour Galliano onto Seagram's Banana Liqueur, then float cream. Optional to stir.

GLASS: Cordial (Lexington)

INGREDIENTS:

15ml Seagram's Banana Liqueur
15ml Galliano
 7ml Cream

TECHNIQUE: Shoot

COMMENTS: This creamy banana ride you won't forget.

JAPANESE SLIPPER

METHOD: Layer Triple Sec onto the Melon then float the Lemon juice. Optional to Stir

GLASS: Tall Dutch Cordial

INGREDIENTS:

20ml Seagram's Melon Liqueur
15ml Seagram's Triple Sec *
10ml Lemon juice

TECHNIQUE: Shoot

COMMENTS: Elegant and refreshing. Precision is required with measurements. To revive failing confidence and replenish that special feeling.
* Cointreau may be substituted for Triple Sec.

JAWBREAKER

METHOD: Pour Apricot Brandy then drop Tabasco Sauce.

GLASS: Whisky shot

INGREDIENTS:

45ml Apricot Brandy
4-5 drops Tabasco Sauce

TECHNIQUE: Shoot

COMMENTS: Grit your teeth after this shot, then slowly open your mouth.

JUMPING JACK FLASH

METHOD: Layer in order.

GLASS: Whisky Shot

INGREDIENTS:

15ml Tia Maria
15ml Coruba Rum
15ml Jack Daniels

TECHNIQUE: Shoot

COMMENTS: Thrill seeking Jack Daniels and his accomplices await this opportunity to shudder your soul.

JUMPING MEXICAN

METHOD: Layer in order.

GLASS: Whisky Shot

INGREDIENTS:
22ml Kahlua
22ml Cougar Bourbon

TECHNIQUE: Shoot

COMMENTS: Jump into Mexico's favourite pastime and bounce back into the party. For those keen on the Mexican Hat Dance.

KAMIKAZE SHOOTER

METHOD: Layer the Cointreau onto Vodka, float the lemon juice, then optional to stir.

GLASS: Whisky Shot

INGREDIENTS:

20ml Finlandia Vodka
15ml Cointreau*
10ml Lemon Juice

TECHNIQUE: Shoot

COMMENTS: Maintain freshness for large volumes by adding strained egg white. Mix in a jug and keep refrigerated. The traditional Kamikaze cocktail has the addition of Lime cordial, it is shaken over ice, strained and then served in a 140ml Cocktail Glass.
*Seagram's Triple Sec may be substituted for Cointreau.

K.G.B. SHOOTER

METHOD: Layer in order.

GLASS: Cordial (Lexington)

INGREDIENTS:

12ml Kahlua
12ml Grand Marnier
12ml Baileys Irish Cream

TECHNIQUE: Shoot

COMMENTS: Grand Marnier adds an orange twist to the Kahlua and Baileys Irish Cream. The traditional K.G.B. cocktail is built over ice with greater volume of ingredient. It is normally served in a 140ml Old Fashioned Spirit Glass.

KOOL AID

METHOD: Layer in order.

GLASS: Cordial (Lexington)

INGREDIENTS:

10ml Seagram's Melon Liqueur
15ml Amaretto di Saronno
12ml Karloff Vodka

TECHNIQUE: Shoot

COMMENTS: A familiar mix with various names. Amaretto's caramel lacing prevents overheating.

LADY THROAT KILLER

METHOD: Layer in order.

GLASS: Tall Dutch Cordial

INGREDIENTS:
20ml Kahlua
15ml Seagram's Melon Liqueur
10ml Frangelico Hazelnut Liqueur

TECHNIQUE: Shoot

COMMENTS: This superb mixture offers an exquisite after-taste. One of my favourite Shooters.

LAMBADA

METHOD: Layer in order.

GLASS: Whisky Shot

INGREDIENTS:
15ml Mango Liqueur
15ml Opal Nera
15ml Pepe Lopez Tequila

TECHNIQUE: Shoot

COMMENTS: Wiggle your way to the bar and order the latest liqueur, Opal Nera. Both the dance and the Shooter will excite your partner.

LASER BEAM

METHOD: Layer in order

GLASS: Cordial (Lexington)

INGREDIENTS:
22ml Kahlua
15ml Galliano

TECHNIQUE: Shoot

COMMENTS: Your palate is illuminated on this celestial journey!

LICK SIP SUCK

METHOD: Pour

GLASS: Whisky Shot

INGREDIENTS:

    30ml El Toro Tequila
    Lemon in quarters or slices
    Salt

TECHNIQUE: On the flat piece of skin between the base of your thumb and index finger, place a pinch of salt. Place a quarter of the lemon by you on the bar. Lick the salt off your hand, shoot the Tequila and then suck the lemon.

COMMENTS: This famous method yields the utmost enjoyment from Tequila. Delicious!

MARC'S RAINBOW

METHOD: Layer in order.

GLASS: Whisky Shot

INGREDIENTS:

7ml Kahlua
8ml Seagram's Melon Liqueur
8ml Malibu
7ml Seagram's Banana Liqueur
8ml Galliano
7ml Grand Marnier

TECHNIQUE: Shoot

COMMENTS: One of Melbourne's best shooter recipes. Discover the pot of gold at the end of the rainbow.

MARGARITA SHOOTER

METHOD: Layer El Toro Tequila onto Cointreau, float lemon juice then dash the lime juice.

GLASS: Whisky Shot

INGREDIENTS:

15ml Cointreau*
15ml El Toro Tequila
10ml Lemon juice
5ml Lime juice

TECHNIQUE: Shoot.

COMMENTS: Everyone should take this plunge. Lemon and Lime neutralise the acid. This Shooter is similar to the traditional Margarita cocktail, which is of greater volume, shaken over ice and served in a salt rimmed Champagne Saucer.

*Seagram's Triple Sec may be substituted for Cointreau

MARTIAN HARD ON

METHOD: Layer in order.

GLASS: Tall Dutch Cordial

INGREDIENTS:

15ml Seagram's Dark Creme de Cacao
15ml Seagram's Melon Liqueur
15ml Baileys Irish Cream

TECHNIQUE: Shoot

COMMENTS: When you are a little green about the facts of life.

MELON SPLICE

METHOD: Layer in order.

GLASS: Tall Dutch Cordial

INGREDIENTS:

    15ml Seagram's Melon Liqueur
    15ml Galliano
    15ml Seagram's Coconut Liqueur

TECHNIQUE: Shoot

COMMENTS: Synonymous with Sunday strolls and ice-cream. Flakes of ice may be sprinkled to chill.

MIDORI SOUR

METHOD: Pour the Grenadine or Raspberry Cordial into the Midori, then float the lemon juice.

GLASS: Tall Dutch Cordial

INGREDIENTS:

30ml Midori*
5ml Grenadine or Raspberry Cordial
10ml Lemon juice

TECHNIQUE: Shoot

COMMENTS: Better than freshly squeezed orange juice this shooter has rejuvenating qualities for early morning revivals.

*Midori may be substituted with Seagram's Melon Liqueur.

NUDE BOMB

METHOD: Layer in order.

GLASS: Cordial (Embassy)

INGREDIENTS:

10ml Kahlua
10ml Seagram's Banana Liqueur
10ml Amaretto di Saronno

TECHNIQUE: Shoot

COMMENTS: Especially created for toga-parties and skinny-dipping.

ORGASM SHOOTER

METHOD: Layer in order.

GLASS: Whisky Shot

INGREDIENTS:

22ml Cointreau*
22ml Baileys Irish Cream

TECHNIQUE: Shoot

COMMENTS: After the first one, you most certainly will want another. The Shooter method is different to the traditional Orgasm cocktail, which is a longer drink, built over ice and served in a 210ml Old Fashioned Spirit Glass
*Seagram's Triple Sec may be substituted for Cointreau.

OYSTER SHOOTER

METHOD: Pour tomato juice onto the Smirnoff Vodka, float the cocktail sauce, dash sauces to taste and drop in oyster.

GLASS: Cordial (Embassy)

INGREDIENTS:

10ml Smirnoff Vodka
10ml Tomato juice
5ml Cocktail sauce (recipe page 10)
Worcestershire sauce to taste
Tabasco sauce to taste
1 Fresh oyster

TECHNIQUE: Shoot

COMMENTS: An early morning wake-up call, replenishing energy lost the night before. Also referred to as a Heart Starter.

PASSION JUICE

METHOD: Layer in order. Optional to stir.

GLASS: Whisky Shot

INGREDIENTS:

    20ml Seagram's Orange Curacao
    10ml Seagram's Cherry Brandy
    15ml Freshly squeezed Orange
         or Lemon juice

TECHNIQUE: Shoot

COMMENTS: A bitter sweet lift by garnishing liqueur passion with juices.

PEACH TREE BAY

METHOD: Layer the Pimm's onto the Peachtree Schnapps, then drop Green Creme de Menthe.

GLASS: Tall Dutch Cordial

INGREDIENTS:
25ml Peachtree Schnapps
15ml Pimm's No.1 Cup
5ml Seagram's Green Creme de Menthe

TECHNIQUE: Shoot

COMMENTS: Conjuring an image of uninhabited places, cool refreshing Pimm's is minted with Green Creme de Menthe.

PEACHY BUM

METHOD: Layer in order.

GLASS: Tall Dutch Cordial

INGREDIENTS:

20ml Mango Liqueur
15ml Peachtree Schnapps
10ml Cream

TECHNIQUE: Shoot

COMMENTS: Delightfully enriched and mellowed by fresh cream.

PEARL NECKLACE

METHOD: Layer in order.

GLASS: Cordial (Embassy)

INGREDIENTS:

15ml Seagram's Melon Liqueur
15ml Pimm's No. 1 Cup

TECHNIQUE: Shoot

COMMENTS: A dash of lemonade dilutes the zappy after-taste.

PERFECT MATCH

METHOD: Layer in order.

GLASS: Cordial (Lexington)

INGREDIENTS:

18ml Parfait Amour
18ml Malibu

TECHNIQUE: Shoot

COMMENTS: Parfaits (Perfect), Amour (Love), proposes future happiness and togetherness under Malibu's exotic veil.

PIPSQUEAK

METHOD: Layer in order, then stir.

GLASS: Cordial (Lexington)

INGREDIENTS:
20ml Frangelico Hazelnut Liqueur
10ml Smirnoff Vodka
7ml Lemon juice

TECHNIQUE: Shoot

COMMENTS: Another favourite of mine. A quaint appetiser before dinner.

RABBIT-PUNCH

METHOD: Pour in order then layer Baileys Irish Cream.

GLASS: Whisky Shot

INGREDIENTS:

    10ml Campari
    10ml Seagram's Dark Creme de Cacao
    10ml Malibu
    15ml Baileys Irish Cream

TECHNIQUE: Shoot

COMMENTS: Baileys Irish Cream assures credibility and its softness will subtly inflict a powerful jab to wake you up and keep you on the hop!

READY, SET, GO!

METHOD: Layer in order.

GLASS : Tall Dutch Cordial

INGREDIENTS:

15ml Seagram's Strawberry Liqueur
15ml Seagram's Banana Liqueur
15ml Seagram's Melon Liqueur

TECHNIQUE: Suction Straw-shoot

COMMENTS: Similar to a Traffic Light, with added sweetness – almost a fermented fruit salad.

RED INDIAN

METHOD: Layer in order.

GLASS: Cordial (Lexington)

INGREDIENTS:

10ml Seagram's Dark Creme de Cacao
12ml Peachtree Schnapps
15ml Canadian Club

TECHNIQUE: Shoot

COMMENTS: Dark Creme de Cacao ripens the Peachtree to tantalise. CC takes the scalp!

RUSTY NAIL

METHOD: Layer in order.

GLASS: Cordial (Embassy)

INGREDIENTS:

15ml Black Douglas Scotch
15ml Drambuie

TECHNIQUE: Shoot

COMMENTS: A pillow-softener, though this age-old blend will never cause fatigue. As a Shooter, great as "one for the road". The traditional cocktail is normally built over ice, in a 210ml Old Fashioned Spirit Glass.

SAMBUCA SHAKER

METHOD: Pour Sambuca then light

GLASS: Wine Goblet

INGREDIENTS:

30-45ml Sambuca Romana

TECHNIQUE: Cup your hand entirely over the rim while it flames, creating suction. Shake the glass, place under your nose, take hand from glass to inhale the fumes, then shoot.

COMMENTS: Everybody shake to this latest fad. The wider the rim the easier suction.

SCREAMING DEATH SHOOTER

METHOD: Layer in the above order. Lighting optional.

GLASS: Tall Dutch Cordial

INGREDIENTS:

15ml Kahlua
10ml Early Times Bourbon
10ml DOM Benedictine
5ml Jack Daniels
5ml Bundaberg OP

TECHNIQUE: Shoot while flaming.

COMMENTS: The pinnacle of endurance. Double layers of flammable fuel cushioned in ascending order by Kahlua, Bourbon and Benedictine, which sweetly numbs any pain. It's truth and dare.

SCREWDRIVER SHOOTER

METHOD: Layer in order.

GLASS: Whisky Shot

INGREDIENTS:

15ml Seagram's Orange Curacao
30ml Karloff Vodka

TECHNIQUE: Shoot

COMMENTS: Add a dash of Peachtree Schnapps and it's known as a 'Fuzzy Navel'. The Shooter mix departs from the traditionl Screwdriver cocktail by the substitution of Orange Curacao for Orange Juice. The cocktail is also built over ice in a 210ml Old Fashioned Spirit Glass.

SEX IN THE SNOW

METHOD: Pour in order, then stir.

GLASS: Cordial (Lexington)

INGREDIENTS:

12ml Seagram's Triple Sec
12ml Malibu
12ml Aphrodite Ouzo

TECHNIQUE: Straw shoot

COMMENTS: The sub-zero temperature of this combination is chillingly refreshing when drunk through a straw.

SHERBERT BURP

METHOD: Pour Strawberry Liqueur then top up with Champagne.

GLASS: Tall Dutch Cordial

INGREDIENTS:
15ml Seagram's Strawberry Liqueur
30ml Mumm Cordon Rouge Champagne

TECHNIQUE: Shoot

COMMENTS: Change the colour of your burp with any flavoured liqueur. Even better, multi-colour it!

SIDECAR SHOOTER

METHOD: Layer Cointreau onto Brandy, float lemon juice, then optional to stir.

GLASS: Cordial (Lexington)

INGREDIENTS:

12ml Chatelle Napoleon Brandy
15ml Cointreau*
10ml Lemon juice

TECHNIQUE: Shoot

COMMENTS: This old-fashioned, lemon-barley refreshment, filtered through Cointreau and lightly tanned with Brandy, restores your zest for life. A slightly different mix to the traditional Sidecar cocktail, which is shaken over ice and served in a 90ml Cocktail Glass.

*Cointreau may be substituted with Seagram's Triple Sec.

SLAMMER

METHOD: Pour and slam.

GLASS: Whisky Shot

INGREDIENTS:

    40ml Pepe Lopez Tequila
    5ml Soda water, lemonade
        or ginger ale

TECHNIQUE: Shoot or lick, sip and suck.

COMMENTS: No party is complete without one! The mixer carbonates the Tequila which fizzes when slammed. Cinzano Dry Vermouth can be substituted if mixers are unavailable. Based on the Tequilla Slammer cocktail.

SLIPPERY NIPPLE

METHOD: Layer in order.

GLASS: Tall Dutch Cordial

INGREDIENTS:

30ml Sambuca de Romana
15ml Baileys Irish Cream

TECHNIQUE: Shoot

COMMENTS: One of the originals, very well received. Cream floated on the Baileys becomes a 'Pregnant Slippery Nipple'. Grand Marnier included makes a 'Slipadicthome'.

SNAKE-BITE

METHOD: Layer in order, then light.

GLASS: Cordial (Embassy)

INGREDIENTS:

20ml Kahlua
10ml Green Chartreuse

TECHNIQUE: Straw shoot while flaming.

COMMENTS: Score this shooter ten out of ten. Drink quickly or the straw will melt.

SPANISH FLY

METHOD: Pour in order.

GLASS: Whisky Shot

INGREDIENTS:

10ml Cinzano Bianco Vermouth
15ml Tequila Pepe Lopez
20ml Ballantines Scotch

TECHNIQUE: Tandem

COMMENTS: No, it's not what you're twinkling eye and devious smirk assumes ... it's better. A guaranteed survival capsule, capable of producing fantasies beyond those Spain is famous for.

STRAWBERRY CREAM

METHOD: Layer in order.

GLASS: Cordial (Embassy)

INGREDIENTS:

20ml Seagram's Strawberry Liqueur
10ml Cream

TECHNIQUE: Shoot

COMMENTS: Begin your trip to the "World of Shooters" with this one. Cream acts as a buffer to entice the nervous and inexperienced. Strawberries calm what was needless concern.

SUCTION CUP

METHOD: Layer the Melon onto Vodka, then pour Blue Curacao.

GLASS: Cordial (Lexington)

INGREDIENTS:

20ml Finlandia Vodka
10ml Seagram's Melon Liqueur
7ml Seagram's Blue Curacao

TECHNIQUE: Suction-straw shoot.

COMMENTS: A supersonic vacuum results from this drinking method.

SUITOR

METHOD: Pour in order.

GLASS: Cordial (Lexington)

INGREDIENTS:

10ml Drambuie*
10ml Grand Marnier
10ml Baileys Irish Cream
 7ml Milk

TECHNIQUE: Shoot

COMMENTS: Milk inclusion coddles a cool moment, resettles anxieties when approaching the fair sex, guaranteed to excite romance.
*Drambuie may be substituted with Lochan Ora.

SUKIYAKI

METHOD: Layer in order.

GLASS: Cordial (Embassy)

INGREDIENTS:
    10ml Mango Liqueur
    10ml Apricot Brandy
    10ml Malibu

TECHNIQUE: Shoot

COMMENTS: Essential starter for a superb Japanese banquet.

THE DAY AFTER

METHOD: Layer Tequila onto Cointreau, drop the Blue Curacao, then layer Green Chartreuse and light.

GLASS: Cordial (Embassy)

INGREDIENTS:

10ml Cointreau*
10ml El Toro Tequila
 5 drops Seagram's Blue Curacao
10ml Green Chartreuse

TECHNIQUE: Shoot after flame extinguished.

COMMENTS: An upside down day!

*Cointreau may be substituted with Seagram's Triple Sec.

TICKLED PINK

METHOD: Pour White Creme de Menthe followed by a dash of Grenadine or Raspberry Cordial.

GLASS: Whisky Shot

INGREDIENTS:
40ml Seagram's White Creme de Menthe
5ml Grenadine or Raspberry Cordial

TECHNIQUE: Shoot

COMMENTS: For those who are bashful when complimented.

TOWERING INFERNO

METHOD: Layer in order, then light.

GLASS: Cordial (Embassy)

INGREDIENTS:
10ml Gilbey's Gin
10ml Seagram's Triple Sec
10ml Green Chartreuse

TECHNIQUE: Shoot while flaming.

COMMENTS: Designed to set the night on fire.

TRAFFIC LIGHT

METHOD: Layer in order, then light.

GLASS: Tall Dutch Cordial

INGREDIENTS:
10ml Seagram's Strawberry Liqueur
10ml Galliano
25ml Green Chartreuse

TECHNIQUE: Suction-straw shoot.

COMMENTS: Ready set go! Substitute Seagram's Banana Liqueur for Galliano and Seagram's Melon Liqueur for Green Chartreuse, for those with a sweet tooth.

103

TWAIN'S ORGASM

METHOD: Layer in order.

GLASS : Cordial (Embassy)

INGREDIENTS:

20ml Peachtree Schnapps
10ml Baileys Irish Cream

TECHNIQUE: Shoot

COMMENTS: Travel down the Mississippi where Huckleberry Finn once played. Also known as a 'P.B.'

U-TURN

METHOD: Layer in order.

GLASS: Whisky Shot

INGREDIENTS:

15ml Seagram's Banana Liqueur
30ml Tia Maria

TECHNIQUE: Shoot

COMMENTS: The Banana offers the curve yet its Tia Maria that sends you around the bend. A complete change of direction.

VIBRATOR

METHOD: Layer in order.

GLASS : Cordial (Embassy)

INGREDIENTS:
10ml Baileys Irish Cream
20ml Southern Comfort

TECHNIQUE: Shoot

COMMENTS : Batteries are not required for this stimulating and pulsating comfort.

VIOLET SLUMBER

METHOD: Layer in order

GLASS: Cordial (Lexington)

INGREDIENTS:

15ml Malibu
12ml Parfait Amour
10ml Orange juice

TECHNIQUE: Shoot

COMMENTS: Pretty to look at, better to drink, but don't slumber on this number.

VODKA-TINI

METHOD: Pour in order, then stir.

GLASS: Cordial (Embassy)

INGREDIENTS:

25ml Smirnoff Vodka
5ml Cinzano Dry Vermouth

TECHNIQUE: Shoot

COMMENTS: No olive is required. Preferably served chilled.

WATER-BUBBA

METHOD: Pour Advocaat into Cherry Advocaat, then layer the Blue Curacao.

GLASS: Cordial (Lexington)

INGREDIENTS:

15ml Seagram's Cherry Advocaat
10ml Seagram's Advocaat
12ml Seagram's Blue Curacao

TECHNIQUE: Shoot

COMMENTS: The Advocaat resembles an egg yolk, with veins of Cherry Advocaat. Also known as an 'Unborn Baby'.

WHITE DEATH

METHOD: Layer in order, then light.

GLASS: Tall Dutch Cordial

INGREDIENTS:

15ml Gilbey's Gin
15ml Pepe Lopez Tequila
15ml Sambuca Romana

TECHNIQUE: Shoot after flame is extinguished.

COMMENTS: Be careful, sometimes clear fluid can be violent.

ZOWIE

METHOD: Layer in order.

GLASS: Tall Dutch Cordial

INGREDIENTS:

15ml Seagram's Banana Liqueur
15ml Baileys Irish Cream
15ml Malibu

TECHNIQUE: Shoot

COMMENTS: An exotic exclamation of surprise! Almost a banana-coconut smoothie.

Acknowledgements
This book is proudly sponsored by the following companies.
Libbey Glassware Pty Ltd
Suppliers of: a wide range of quality glassware to the retail and hospitality trades.
Milne Liquor Agencies (a division of Swift & Moore Pty Ltd) 8 Egerton Street, Silverwater,
NSW 2141
Telephone: (02) 647 1599 Fax: (02) 648 1257
Suppliers of:
Aphrodite Ouzo, Ballantine's Scotch Whisky, Early Times Bourbon Coruba Jamaican Rum, Pepe Lopez Tequila, Gilbey's Gin, Milne Brandy, Courvoisier Cognac, Smirnoff Vodka , Canadian Club, Grand Marnier, Tia Maria, Moet & Chandon Champagne, Kahlua and many other fine wines, spirits and liqueurs.
Seagram Australia Pty Ltd
32 Jasmine Street, Botany, NSW 2019
Telephone: (02) 695 3999 Fax: (02) 666 5375
Suppliers of:
Seagram's Liqueurs, Martell Cognac, Amaretto di Saronno, Vandermint, Lochan Ora, Sabra, Karloff Vodka, Finlandia Vodka, Captain Morgan Rum, El Toro Tequila, Kirsch, Mumm Cordon Rouge Champagne, Cougar Bourbon, Chatelle Napoleon Brandy, The Black Douglas Scotch Whisky, Chivas Regal and a wide range of other quality wines, liqueurs and spirits
Remy Blass & Associates Pty. Ltd.
272 Pacific Highway, Crow's Nest, N.S.W. 2065
Telephone: (02) 436 0888
Suppliers of:
Galliano, Amaretto di Galliano, Sambuca di Galliano, Passoa, Cointreau and many other fine wines and spirits.
Alpen Products Pty. Ltd.
130 Old Pittwater Road, Brookvale N.S.W. 2100
Telephone: 905 7603 Fax: 905 7621
Suppliers of:
Party Novelties, Decorations, Toothpicks, Swizzle Sticks and other Drink Accessories.
Posi-Pour Wholesalers Pty. Ltd.
170 Banksia Street, Pagewood N.S.W. 2035
Telephone: 316 8245 Fax: 316 8251
Suppliers of:
Posi-Pour pourers and Posi-Pour portion control pourers.

INDEX

ALABAMA SLAMMER	17	G.A.S.	45
Alcohol Needed	10	Glasses	9
Alcohol recommended		GOLDEN	
for a cocktail bar	11	CADILLAC SHOOTER	46
ATOMIC BOMB	18	GREEK GOD	47
B & B SHOOTER	19	GREEN SLIME	48
B-52 SHOOTER	20	HALF NELSON	49
BEE STING	21	HARBOUR LIGHTS	50
Black Pearl	22	HARD ON	51
BLACK RUSSIAN		Heart Starter	75
SHOOTER	22	HELLRAISER	52
BLOOD BATH	23	Helpful Hints	7
BLOW JOB	24	HIGH AND DRY	53
BRAIN DAMAGE	25	Ice	8
BRAVE BULL	26	INKAHLUARABLE	54
Building	5	Introduction	4
CALYPSO	27	IRISH FLAG	55
CHASTITY BELT	28	ITALIAN STALLION	56
CHERRY RIPE	29	JAPANESE SLIPPER	57
CHILLI SHOT	30	JAWBREAKER	58
Chilling	8	JUMPING JACK FLASH	59
CHOCOLATE NOUGAT	31	JUMPING MEXICAN	60
COATHANGER	32	KAMIKAZE SHOOTER	61
COURTING PENELOPE	33	K.G.B. SHOOTER	62
DARK SUNSET	34	KOOL AID	63
Dash	6	LADY THROAT KILLER	64
Description of		LAMBADA	65
Liqueurs and Spirits	12	LASER BEAM	66
DEVIL'S HANDBRAKE	35	Layering	6
DIRTY ORGASM	36	Lighting	6
DOUBLE DATE	37	LICK SIP SUCK	67,7
Drinking Methods	7	MARC'S RAINBOW	68
Dropping	7	MARGARITA SHOOTER	69
Equipment Required for		MARTIAN HARD ON	70
Shooters	10	MELON SPLICE	71
FIZZY RUSH	38	Methods of	
FLAMING		Mixing Shooters	5
LAMBORGHINI		MIDORI SOUR	72
SHOOTER	39	Non Alcoholic Ingredients	10
FLAMING LOVER	40	NUDE BOMB	73
FLAMING SAMBUCA	41	ORGASM SHOOTER	74
Floating	6	Other Liqueurs	13
FREDDIE FUD PUCKER	42	OYSTER SHOOTER	75
FRUIT TINGLE	43	PASSION JUICE	76
Fuzzy Navel	88	P.B.	104
GALLIANO HOT SHOT	44	PEACH TREE BAY	77
Garnishes	8	PEACHY BUM	78

113

PEARL NECKLACE	79	SNAKE-BITE	94
PERFECT MATCH	80	SPANISH FLY	95
PIPSQUEAK	81	Stirring	5,6
Pouring	5,6	Straw Shoot	7
Pregnant Slippery Nipple	93	STRAWBERRY CREAM	96
RABBIT-PUNCH	82	SUCTION CUP	97
Rattlesnake	24	Suction Straw Shoot	7
READY,SET,GO!	83	SUITOR	98
Recipe for Cocktail Sauce	8	SUKIYAKI	99
RED INDIAN	84	Tandem	7
Responsible Drinking	5	Techniques for making shooters	6
RUSTY NAIL	85	THE DAY AFTER	100
SAMBUCA SHAKER	86	TICKLED PINK	101
SCREAMING DEATH SHOOTER	87	Tilting	6
Screaming Orgasm	36	T.K.O.	26
SCREWDRIVER SHOOTER	88	TOWERING INFERNO	102
		TRAFFIC LIGHT	103
SEX IN THE SNOW	89	TWAIN'S ORGASM	104
SHERBERT BURP	90	U-TURN	105
Shoot	7	Unborn Baby	109
Shoot While Flaming	7	VIBRATOR	106
Shooter Time	5	VIOLET SLUMBER	107
SIDECAR SHOOTER	91	VODKA-TINI	108
SLAMMER	92	WATER-BUBBA	109
Slamming	6	WHITE DEATH	110
Slipadicthome	93	ZOWIE	111
SLIPPERY NIPPLE	93		

HOME USER EASY INDEX

Advocaat: Brain Damage, Violet Slumber, Water-Bubba
Amaretto di Galliano: G.A.S.
Amaretto di Saronno: Alabama Slammer, Nude Bomb, Kool Aid
Apricot Brandy: Fizzy Rush, Jawbreaker, Sukiyaki
Baileys Irish Cream: B-52, Blow-Job, Calypso, Chastity Belt, Chocolate Nougat, Dirty Orgasm, Irish Flag, KGB, Martian Hard-On, Orgasm, Rabbit Punch, Rattlesnake, Slippery Nipple, Slipadicthome, Suitor, Twain's Orgasm, Vibrator, Zowie
Banana Liqueur: Brain Damage, Devil's Handbrake, Hard On, Italian Stallion, Marc's Rainbow, Nude Bomb, Ready, Set, Go, U-Turn, Zowie
Blue Curacao: Fruit Tingle, Suction Cup, The Day After, Water-Bubba
Brandy (Chatelle Napoleon): Irish Flag, Sidecar, B&B
Brandy (Milne): Cocktail Sauce
Bundaberg Overproof Rum: Screaming Death Shooter
Bourbon (Cougar): Jumping Mexican

Bourbon (Early Times): Screaming Death Shooter
Campari: Rabbit Punch
Canadian Club: Red Indian
Champagne: Fizzy Rush
Champagne (Mumm Cordon Rouge): Sherbert Burp
Cherry Advocaat: Cherry Ripe, Water-Bubba
Cherry Brandy: Devil's Handbrake, Passion Juice
Cinzano Bianco Vermouth: High and Dry, Spanish Fly
Cinzano Dry Vermouth: High and Dry, Vodka-Tini
Cinzano Rosso Vermouth: Blood Bath, Cherry Ripe
Coconut Liqueur: Melon Splice
Cointreau: B-52, Coathanger, Dirty Orgasm, Kamikaze, Margarita Shooter, Orgasm, The Day After,
Cognac (Martell): Courting Penelope, B&B.
Coruba Rum UP: Calypso, Jumping Jack Flash
Dark Creme de Cacao: Black Pearl, Dark Sunset, Martian Hard-On, Rabbit Punch, Red Indian
DOM Benedictine: B&B, Chocolate Nougat, Double Date, Pipsqueak, Screaming Death Shooter
Drambuie: Rusty Nail, Suitor
Frangelico Hazelnut Liqueur: Chastity Belt, Chocolate Nougat, Lady Throat Killer, Pipsqueak
Galliano: Dirty Orgasm, Flaming Lamborghini, Freddie Fud Pucker, G.A.S., Galliano Hot Shot, Golden Cadillac, Italian Stallion, Laser Beam, Marc's Rainbow, Melon Splice, Traffic Light
Gin: (Gilbey's):Towering Inferno, White Death
Gin, (Seagram's London Dry): Alabama Slammer, Atomic Bomb
Grand Marnier: Courting Penelope, Half Nelson, Inkahluarable, KGB, Marc's Rainbow, Slipadicthome, Suitor
Green Chartreuse: Flaming Lamborghini, Harbour Lights, Rattlesnake, Snake-Bite, The Day After, Towering Inferno, Traffic Light
Green Creme de Menthe: Blow Job, Half Nelson, Irish Flag, Peach Tree Bay, Rattlesnake
Jack Daniels: Jumping Jack Flash, Screaming Death Shooter
Kahlua: B-52, Black Russian, Brave Bull, Cherry Ripe, Flaming Lamborghini, Harbour Lights, Hard On, Inkahluarable, Jumping Mexican, KGB, Lady Throat Killer, Laser Beam, Marc's Rainbow, Nude Bomb, Screaming Death Shooter, Snake-Bite, TKO.
Lochan Ora: Drambuie
Malibu: Brain Damage, Calypso, Dark Sunset, Marc's Rainbow, Perfect Match, Rabbit Punch, Sex in The Snow, Sukiyaki, Violet Slumber, Zowie
Mango Liqueur: Devil's Handbrake, Fruit Tingle, Lambada, Peachy Bum, Sukiyaki

Melon Liqueur: Double Date, Green Slime, Japanese Slipper, Kool Aid, Lady Throat Killer, Marc's Rainbow, Martian Hard-On, Pearl Necklace, Melon Splice, Ready, Set, Go, Suction Cup,
Midori : Midori Sour, Hellraiser
Opal Nera: Lambada, Hellraiser
Orange Curacao: Freddie Fud Pucker, Fuzzy Navel, Passion Juice, Screwdriver
Ouzo: (Aphrodite) Greek God, Sex in The Snow, TKO
Parfait Amour: Brain Damage, Perfect Match, Violet Slumber
Peachtree Schnapps: Fuzzy Navel, Peach Tree Bay, Peachy Bum, Twains Orgasm, Red Indian
Pernod: Greek God
Pimm's: Pearl Necklace, Peach Tree Bay
Sambuca di Galliano: G.A.S.
Sambuca Romana: Flaming Sambuca, Sambuca Shaker, Slipadicthome, Slippery Nipple, White Death,
Sambuca (Seagram's): Flaming Lover, Harbour Lights
Scotch (Ballantines): Spanish Fly
Scotch (Black Douglas): Rusty Nail
Southern Comfort: Alabama Slammer, Vibrator
Strawberry Liqueur: Blood Bath, Half-Nelson, Strawberry Cream, Hellraiser, Ready, Set, Go, Sherbert Burp, Traffic Light
Tequila (El Toro): Bee Sting, Freddie Fud Pucker, Lick Sip Suck, Margarita Shooter, The Day After.
Tequila (Pepe Lopez): Bee Sting, Blood Bath, Brave Bull, High and Dry, Slammer, Spanish Fly, TKO, White Death, Lambada, Coathanger
Tia Maria: Atomic Bomb, Black Pearl, Chastity Belt, Jumping Jack Flash, U-Turn
Triple Sec (Seagram's): Flaming Lover, Inkahluarable, Japanese Slipper, Kamikaze, Sex in the Snow, Towering Inferno
Vodka (Smirnoff): Black Pearl, Black Russian, Chilli Shot, Fuzzy Navel, Oyster Shooter, Pipsqueak, Vodka-Tini.,
Vodka (Karloff): Green Slime, Kool Aid, Screwdriver
Vodka (Finlandia): Suction Cup, Kamikaze,
White Creme de Cacao: Golden Cadillac
White Creme de Menthe: Double Date, Fizzy Rush, Tickled Pink
Yellow Chartreuse: Bee Sting

This book is stocked by all good booksellers and liquor retailers, however, if you have difficulty obtaining additional copies then please return this order form. Other books in the 101 Series may be ordered using this form, just note title and send payment for the required amount. All books in the 101 Series are $9.95 plus $1.50 P & P. Note that for orders of more than five copies no postage or packaging is payable as at 31st December 1991 (Prices subject to change without notice)

R & R Publishing, P.O. Box 1071, Epping, NSW 2121
12 Treeview Place, Epping, NSW 2121

Telephone Orders: (02) 876 5958 Fax (02) 876 3782

Please send me .... copy/ies of book/s as marked @ $9.95 plus $1.50 post and packaging per copy. Find enclosed my cheque/money order for $............. or charge my credit card

EXPIRY DATE .... SIGNATURE ....

BANKCARD/MASTERCARD/VISA

| | | | | |-| | | | |-| | | | |

	101 Shooters
	101 Cocktails
	101 Mocktails

NAME: _____

ADDRESS _____

_____ P/CODE _____